The Diary I Couldn't Keep

FROM ASHES TO INK

Jocelyn Broadnax AKA Fierce Rebel

BookLeaf
Publishing

India | USA | UK

Made with ❤ on the BookLeaf Publishing Platform
www.bookleafpub.in
www.bookleafpub.com

Dedication

I dedicate this book to all the versions of myself that lie within the pages of my past journals. To the many pieces of myself that I had to eulogize with my pen for them to fall away from my reality. May they rest in peace knowing that their sacrifice birthed the greatest resurrection of my truth. These entries are from different periods in my life, not in any particular order. When I take moments to reflect on my past writings, I tend to feel a mix of emotion. Usually, it was a great glimpse into how much I've grown, or how much more healing was still waiting to be done.

But now it is something more.

Each word, each line, is a timestamp of who I was becoming while trying to remember who I am. This collection is not just a mirror—it's a bridge. Between who I was, who I am, and who I'm still becoming.

I also dedicate this book to the reader. To anyone who finds themselves within these pages. I hope you find comfort in knowing you're not alone in your chaos, whatever that may be. That your transformation—no matter how messy—still counts as evolution. I release these words knowing that this version of me will never reappear again. This farewell is my most sacral offering.

Preface

Finding Strength in Vulnerability

I've always had a naturally expressive personality, able to articulate my thoughts and feelings with ease, especially in spaces where I felt safe. But over time, I encountered situations where the people closest to me used my openness against me. These experiences made me question the value of sharing my deepest thoughts and emotions, leaving me hesitant and guarded.

For years, I wanted to have a platform expressing myself. I wanted to find people like me so they could know as well as I that there are others. Individuals with good hearts, multifaceted minds, versatile spirits looking for a safe space to be free. However, I held back, haunted by past betrayals. I started to believe vulnerability was a weakness—a crack in the armor that could be exploited, a door left ajar for judgment to slip through. I spent so much energy hiding my truths, convinced it was safer to keep them tucked away. But life has a way of forcing us to confront what truly matters, even when we're not ready.

I faced an emergency that turned my life upside down. I

had been having unprotected sex with someone I considered a friend. He had been in my life for almost a year—maybe longer—before we ever crossed that line. I'd never viewed him in a sexual way until one day, during one of our usual nights of drinking and smoking, one thing led to another.

At that point in my life, I had built a wall around myself to avoid the pain that toxic, unhealthy love had brought me in the past. I convinced myself that keeping things casual—an orgasm with someone I liked and trusted— was better than risking the emotional turmoil of a serious relationship. So, after we had sex, I didn't demand anything from him. I didn't ask new questions or redefine our dynamic. We carried on, casually and unprotected, until the day I found out I was pregnant.

When I told him I was pregnant, the conversation quickly spiraled into a mess of gaslighting and excuses. He brought up how his kids were older, how I didn't understand the cost of daycare, and how the baby wasn't conceived under the "right circumstances." He even mentioned the burden of explaining the situation to his other children and their mothers.

Then, he asked me to sign a document that would absolve him of any responsibility. I refused. That's when he made it painfully clear: if I went through with the pregnancy, he would resent me forever and never speak to me again.

I never thought of having kids. Honestly, I believed I couldn't. After so many years of not getting pregnant, it seemed like motherhood wasn't in the cards for me. But then it happened—unexpectedly, at that specific time in my life and with that particular person. Amidst the hurt from his reaction and the heavy reality that I would be facing life as a single mother, I still couldn't shake the feeling that this had happened for a reason. A part of me believed there was meaning in it all—a purpose I hadn't yet fully understood.

I carried that belief with me as I navigated the uncertainty, making it to 20 weeks and five days. But then everything changed. I ended up in the hospital, where I lost my baby and came dangerously close to losing my own life. The days that followed were a blur of pain, fear, and isolation.

Alone in a hospital room at night, staring at the ceiling and wondering if I would survive, I was haunted by regret. Regret for never truly being authentic. For never showing up the way I wanted to in the world. For keeping my poetry, my writings, my thoughts, and my testimony locked away. I had dreamed of building a community where people could thrive together, lifting each other up through shared truths. But I had been too afraid—afraid of judgment, rejection, and the vulnerability it would take to live out loud.

And now, it all seemed so distant. So gone.

I made a promise to myself during those long nights. If I made it through, I wouldn't hesitate to shout my truths from the rooftops. I wouldn't let fear keep me from being who I wanted to be. I vowed to live fully and authentically.

But when the time came—when my health improved, and the chance to speak my truth arrived—I found myself silent. The words slipped away, swallowed by the fear that had long held me captive. What if they judged me? What if my vulnerability made me look weak?

I'm still learning how to push past those fears. What I've come to realize is that vulnerability isn't about being fearless; it's about moving forward despite the fear. It's about opening yourself up, even when you're trembling, and trusting that what you have to share matters.

Vulnerability is what connects us as humans. When I began to share pieces of my story, even just with those closest to me that I KNOW I CAN TRUST, I noticed something profound: people didn't pull away. They leaned in. They shared their own stories, their own struggles. In opening myself up, I found connection, understanding, and strength—not just for myself but for others, too.

Strength isn't about being unbreakable. It's about being brave enough to embrace the cracks and let the light shine through. It's about showing up as your whole self, scars and all, and saying, "This is who I am."

There is power in vulnerability, even when it feels terrifying. Take it one step at a time. Share a piece of your truth with someone you trust. Write it down. Speak it out loud. Let yourself be seen—not as perfect, but as real.

You are not alone. You never were. And the beauty of vulnerability is that it reminds us of that truth. Together, we can build the connections and communities that help us thrive.

Today, I'm stepping into that promise I made in the hospital, and I invite you to join me. Let's shout our truths—not because it's easy, but because it's necessary.

I have a blog website I'm still working on but please visit. It will eventually morph into a collection of my poems, others poetry that choose to post, and full journal entries from the books I pulled these poems from.

www.paradoxicallabyrinth.com

Follow me on Social Media

Personal- sumthin_different_

Fierce Rebel- Associated with my Youtube-
fierce_rebel913

Blog- paradoxicallabyrinth913

Youtube- Fierce Rebel AKA Theeanomaleezclozet

Tiktok- fiercerebel87

Acknowledgements

To my momma, my backbone and my best blessing.
You taught me resilience before I even knew the word
existed.
To my ancestors who walked before me, to my friends
who held space for me, and to every soul who ever
connected with my chaos and my calm — thank you.
To every misfit, truth-teller, and soul-searcher who ever
questioned the rules — you are the heartbeat of this
book.

2017. Depths Uncharted

Pain is the gateway to new perspectives
I've always been a lover of deep things
Things that bring forth emotion, provoke thought, reveal
fears, shed light on ugly truths of reality
I am a bundle of versatility
I am light, dark, rainbows, sunshine, butterflies, moons,
stars, galaxies, and universes
I am words, sentences, paragraphs, pages and books
I am weird, different, paradoxical, an anomaly
I am transparent, open, closed, an introvert, and an
extrovert
I am beauty and I am a fucking mess
Proud to be thee
N when I make my grand exit there will never be
another ME
I am the depth that I search for in movies, books, n
conversations
The journey to me is overwhelming, it's like an endless
maze
A strong ass web that I, the spider engineered with great

precision
N now I'm stuck.
Stuck n challenges
Stuck in action
Stuck in growth
Understanding my misunderstandings
Riding my own waves til I'm tired
Getting carried away in my tides
N drowning in my ocean
Until I learn to swim!

2017. Prayer

Staring at this blank page
Waiting for my thoughts to connect to my fingers so my
pen can bleed my feelings
Searching for a relief, an outburst of emotion
Overflowing...
Once finished this paper will have become a bloody
vessel and my conscious cleared
At least for the moment everything will be still
Peace..... a little slice seems fulfilling to others but I'm
yearning for the whole pie
So let the ink drip from the well of my soul and crowd
this space with all the misunderstandings of my mind
When I reread this later I shall be able to put my life into
perspective
My mind, soul, and heart should align

2018. The Return to Myself

Knowing that I'm destined for greatness I question the
disappointment I cause myself
Mistakes are beyond normal and without failure, how
could I measure my success?
I know my struggles are indeed for a reason and every
mishap planned by the universe
Some lessons I feel are a waste of learning and I walk on
shells trying to stay off that course
But somehow, I find myself digging the same holes
because I find comfort in that space
I pray on a daily then fall off the wagon, Lord knows I
don't need to stay in that place
Funny thing is I search for all these outside extremities
to save me
I've realized when I'm drowning nobody even notices, so
how can they help me?
I'm the water, the harsh waves, the boat, paddle, and the
life jacket
I look to others for justification and reassurance, but I
know what I got

Letting society make me feel as if I've failed as a woman
because I lack a relationship,
sometimes don't want to comb my hair, lay my edges,
and fix my brows
I want to shine from the inside out I just don't know how
This year coming up I promise myself is the year of
greatness
The most connected one I've had since I was born
Where I will search every crevice and corner of my soul
for my beings
Wherever they are hiding, we'll all be free
No more silence, no more choosing when to appear,
which one is good for the moment, while the other
suffers on punishment
We will all flourish together and bring back the original
version of myself
I've been away so long mannn, I don't even know who
I'm staring at,
I have talks in the mirror and I don't even know who's
talking back!
And that's sad!
I look around and think to myself, is everybody going
through this shit?
I know I'm not crazy!
You can be all wrapped in perfection and be pieces of
tidbits of pity
I don't want to be perfect, I just want to find the joy in

me

I want to see the beauty in me at all times
When I'm naked, clothed, painting, playing the guitar,
writing, fucking, or conversing
I want to be the best poem ever written and read
The best literature on the shelf
Not because it overshadowed someone else
But because it has a separate section lying on a lonely
ledge
But attracting people whom know the value.

2017. Anatomy of Destruction

If pain could be measured
I wonder how much mines would weigh
It seems self-inflicted, all I have to do is keep ppl away
No one genuine these days
But I still ask them to stay
Without saying a word, I pulled them in
With my stupidity and low self esteem
And they feed off that shit like leeches
They eat away at my flesh until I'm skin and bone
My soul seeps away through my open wounds
My mind dissipates as thoughts scatter through it
Like roaches on a midnight snack
Meanwhile my ass is about to have a literal heart attack
Sadness overwhelms me
Depression plays tunes on my radio
Anxiety is knocking at my door
And although I'm tired of the pain and stress
My next decision yells
"GIVE ME MORE"

2020. The Person I Can't Reach

I walk beside you daily and still don't know who you are
or what you're doing
I touch your face, pull your hair, read your thoughts, but
still don't understand how you feel
The barriers you've built over the years seems so tough, I
can't pierce it
The map I carry to find you is more like a maze changing
on a consistent basis
I cry tears, build a bridge, and still can't manager to cross
it, seems endless
A battle that I'm not equipped to fight
A puzzle that's missing pieces without the box
A lock that only I hold the key to but buried it so deep in
my past
With no time machine to go back and find it
No drug, alcohol, or magic can help me
It's like being buried alive 6ft deep in your own body
Ppl look at me like I'm crazy when I openly question
whether living or dying makes a difference

Am I losing it, lost, or is everyone else fucked up?
Is it better to be blind or have sight if you still can't see?
Easier to be a child or an adult looking for fairytales but
facing harsh reality?
A play that I can't seem to intercept
A poem that I can't conclude
An illness I can't seem to diagnose

2016. Inside these walls

Hours later, I contradict the promises I made to myself.
Forgive me—
for my flesh controls my next move.
Now the tears rolling down my face
gather in a pool of lies I tell myself.
Why would anyone keep a promise
when I break my own so consistently?

My feelings fall upon deaf ears,
and my heart aches
for someone to hold it tenderly—
to honor its weight.
For it doesn't understand
the pain it carries,
or who was the first
to blame.

2023. Dear Audacity

I heard that song you made—
shit was lame, just like you.
I guess that was your way
of throwing me shade.
Went from coworker,
to friend,
to fuck buddy—
you took your time,
listened to my trauma,
just to plan to become a part of it.
That's weird shit.
Acted like you was a grown ass man,
but ended on some kid shit.
Then you doing podcasts about fatherhood—
that's funny,
but you made it sound lit.
Talk is cheap,
and your words?
They ain't really worth shit.
You say you stand ten toes down,

but just the same as the average statistic.
All that time,
you had a girl—
but was fucking this pussy all crazy,
with a raw dick.
I'm not surprised.
Full circle,
I see all the lies.
Yeah, I can admit—
I ignored all the signs.
Thought I was protecting myself
by not getting attached.
But I was just as fucked up as you
when that test showed positive results.
I didn't understand how or why,
so I took it as a blessing still.
God don't make no mistakes—
but he had to make that lesson real.
It took some time to realize
you was a whole ass snake.
From the start,
your intentions held ill will.
But it's all good—
Karma never fails.
If you thought it was over, baby,
buckle the fuck up.
Ain't no time to chill.

You forgot how in touch I am
with the universe.
This some Queen shit.
I might look like a regular girlie,
but don't get it twisted—
I'm Supreme, BITCH.
Nothing but genuine vibes,
spirit dope,
big-ass heart—
it was really *your* loss.
I'm disgusted—
almost cost me my life.
That bullet was fierce,
thank God I dodged it.
I got caught up on that dick,
and I can't lie—
that was your best trait.
But I didn't ask for that shit.
You could've just left me your homie,
'cause I ain't even look at you like that.
Still, I took the bait.
You caught me when I was trying to heal,
on some vulnerable shit—
I wasn't thinking straight.
Then you talking 'bout
how my friends wanted you—
boy, fuck is you saying?

13

If only you knew.
A big-ass bowl of Wheaties
had to be what you ate.
Fuck is wrong with y'all male Geminis?
Y'all swear y'all so divine.
Bringing up how I was banging *The Weekend* by SZA,
heavy singing the lyrics,
then you wanted to make it real—
by crossing the line.
Everything about you was fake,
acting like you was bossin' and shit.
Whole time,
that wasn't even your whip—
found out it was shorty's ride,
Like... your're really a whole slimmmmeeee
I'm not surprised.
I can pick you out a line up of fuck niggas
a thousand times.
The funny thing is—
you got two daughters.
I can't wait 'til they meet a nigga
who tries to darken their light
that so brightly shines.
Like I said,
Karma is a bitch.
And if she can't reach you,
it's gonna b close

14

You don't need a watch—
you'll never know the time.
But I just wanna take this moment
to say *thank you.*
You was the last one
to ever play in my face—
and with my mind.

2020. Convenient

You say you didn't intend to hurt me,
although you never took precautions to prevent it,
and made no effort to mend it.
I laid down before you
a huge decision,
and I understood your apprehension.
For once, we stood on opposite sides—
we never made anything clear,
never should have crossed the lines.
It's too late for "what ifs."
Can't turn back the hands of time.
Can't act as if nothing happened.
Can't live a lie.
So now what?
You reach out to me,
you spit words,
but never say shit.
You wanna move forward
and think I'm just going to forgive?
As bad as I want to forget,

that situation will be with me
as long as I live.
I birthed a baby
and lost it the same day.
Milk dripping from my breast,
thoughts all over the place,
emotions wouldn't let me rest.
And you were a ghost by choice.
I was dying,
and you left me stanking.
Now, all of a sudden,
you wanna call
and act like you've been thinking
of me?!
How convenient.

2025. The Placenta Still Left Inside Me

I'm trying to understand the feelings I have.
Everything feels so new —
and so old at the same time.
Feeling so close,
yet so far away.
Feeling lighter,
but so heavy.
Encouraged —
but depleted.
So young,
but so old.
So full,
but so empty.
As the tears fall down my face,
I can't even pinpoint the exact reason.
I was just laying in the bed,
so drained...
so tired —
but I can't sleep.

Things to do,
but I can't move.
And I thought back
to the moment I was in the hospital.
I had just birthed my baby.
He was yanked away as soon as he came out —
lungs not yet developed.
I knew he wouldn't make it.
They promised me I'd have time with him.
But they lied.
The same lady I felt was responsible for my loss
reappeared,
and I felt just as uneasy as I did the first time I saw her.
She came in,
asking questions only the medical crew would know
how to answer—
while I was still in the middle of this traumatic
experience.
She stuck her arm inside me,
fingers prying between my uterus and placenta.
I was only twenty weeks and five days.
Of course it wasn't ready to release.
The pain —
the way I screeched.
But I tell this story to explain
how I feel this transition has been.
Just like that day.

After she couldn't remove the placenta,
I went into surgery.
Woke up to a nurse and doctor arguing
about who didn't order my blood transfusion.
As you can imagine —
I was missing a lot.
I remember staring at the clock
and asking God, *"Is this it?"*
I could hear the ticks of my last moments.
I had to stop them and say,
"Can someone just make sure it gets here — and hurry."
There's so much more to this
I can't even get into here.
And maybe I'm getting off track...
or am I?
Days after being released from the hospital,
I had high fevers.
Went back — long story short —
some placenta was left inside of me.
It almost killed me.
And I feel like that's me now —
my current life is that placenta.
Most parts removed,
but the remnants left behind
are causing me to be diseased.
It's so hard to release it.
The more I hold on,

the sadder I become.
The more I try to ignore it,
the louder it becomes.
I always take the harder road.
I don't understand why
I choose pain —
for others,
for things,
for sustainability,
for what?
There's nothing more important than myself.
And the more I connect with her —
the more she desires
what I still refuse
to bring.

Past Time. Different Character, Same Lessons

The next lesson,
the next suffering,
the next pain
that I refuse to let sting me.
This version of me is dead.
I'm sitting here trying to make excuses
for this man and his inconsistent actions
that never have matched his words.
His lack of communication,
acknowledgement,
and accountability
is a testament of the distance
that's always been between us.
I can't strip down to nothing around him—
there is no safety,
and he doesn't hold the pieces
to put me back together.
He doesn't understand my puzzle
and isn't looking for the box.

Such an anomaly—
and that's where we are similar,
but the differences in our definitions
are held in two separate spectrums
of the universe.
If he could, he would—
but he don't,
and hasn't.
But yet I sit
in front of my door,
after driving to pick up food
from someone who loves me,
would be here,
and always shows up for me
no matter our issues—
wanting to return to my home
but hoping he calls me
before my door opens
and feet carry me in.
I'm playing her
and he's playing me.
I'm overcommunicating lies to her
while he's silently telling me the truth.
But I still sit,
waiting and yearning
to service a side of myself
that finds adoration in confusion—

blurs the lines
of sex, intimacy, love, and lust,
wraps it up
and smokes that bitch consciously.
But all the other parts of her
will have to face
the hurtful realities
she's left to deal with.
All I want to be
is aligned—
but somehow
me, she, her
gets separated
when there is a worthless man
in the picture.

2025. Thread by Thread

I'm sitting here trying to dissect my feelings
but I can't even find one to explain,
to dig in to dig up,
to break down n put back together
in a way that I can understand.
I hate when I get to this point,
I go back to a few months ago
when I felt so in tune with myself—
And how once I started going backwards
with my decision making
I began to get scared and judgmental of my actions,
because I know once I pull one string
the rest of me unravels at a pace
that I can't catch it—
and before you know it
my material is scattered
and all that I took the time to develop is gone.
I mean this could be a great thing right?!
I can always recreate a better version,
but I didn't even get a chance

to fully explore the one before—
before I self-sabotaged it,
before I made excuses,
before I forgot the why of my discipline,
of my goals,
of what's needed to accomplish
and the tools that I worked towards
to bring forth what I pray for.
N now I sit, feeling destroyed,
credit down, finances where?!
body still big,
wet coochie with a broken soul
and no safe dick to give it to.
I'm still holding on to my love for self though,
I'm not losing that part
and I hope I never get low enough that it gets there—
but damnnnnnn.. I want to get it right.
I'm tireeeeddddddd of redoing the same lessons,
so tired of starting again,
soooo tired of talking about it,
so tired of the promises
I have yet to keep to me—
the most important person of it allllllllllllllll!!
But I will continue to pour in
and I know clarity will come.
Honestly I don't want to really face the feelings,
the thoughts,

the emotions.
But I can't run from myself forever.
Life has been going so fast recently
that I haven't had much time to sit—
but it's coming,
and when it does
I'll be here to express

2025. 709

This number comes to me multiple times a day
in multiple ways
I correlate it with a person..
one I want to forget
but maybe there is a bigger meaning behind it
One that can't be searched on google or chat gpt
A personal message just for me.
I sit on this plane that has been delayed by two hours
and I'm watching a movie called *Joy Luck Club*
A friendship of four women, going back into their past,
and digging into their daughter's present.
Sharing their stories with them
so they can know how hard it was
to understand their own worth
because from generation to generation,
finding it was harder than just making a choice
and there was no space in their culture for you to have
it.
So they made sure to live a different life..
one where they said less and showed more

and couldn't fathom how the kids still inherited
the worst values in themselves
that they tried to forget.
I find importance in the stories
of the women who came before me
and I wish I got a chance to know
the sum of all the books their lives has written.
But I guess I am the story.
Rewritten time and time again against their will.
I know they would have wanted better.
I can't give up hope on myself
as hard as it is to hold on tight.
It's a challenge to stay on a deeper track
because this surface is slippery
and requires so much of me.
So much of the person I can't choose to be..
To whom much is given much is required.
N what I have is more than any monetary value can
offer.
I have to repeat this to myself.
Like a broken fucking record.
Like how much I repeat the negative words
over my body and my mind.
Like how I repeat bad love decisions
and poor friendships,
like how I repeat repeat and repeat
all that I don't want for myself.

29

Like how 709 repeats itself in my world each day.
I must repeat the love and the strength I have.
One that can be utilized and multiplied like no other
because where it comes from
is a source that can't be destroyed
only magnified.

2024. The Clock Tick Tocs

It's 10:19pm and I have officially been 37 for
Almost 48 hrs. Wow how time flies.
How much the definition of fun changes as the clock
tick tocs at the speed of
What feels like lightning bolts striking fires
To drink feels like consciously consuming poison
Smoking weed feels like brain damage
Trying other drugs gives fear like a death sentence
And all other activities that used to give thrills now
bring chills
and I'm unsure of what to do to celebrate
Food is not a safe space to dwell because I have to be
aware of the decisions made
Keeping my external desires and internal needs at the
forefront of my mind
Oh how responsible am I
These are all protest to the maturity that so selfishly
snuck upon me

2024. Echoes of Change

I'm in this new ERA
I thought transformation was a stop in between
experiences
but I realize it's the backdrop to all the scenes
The seen and unseen with lots of b-roll in the shadows
Every day, hour, min, and sec
is melting into another layer of our existence
and we are echoing the changes with our next step
Whether good or bad.
We don't mind transitions when they are light and fluffy
we don't even know we are indulging in it at all
It's only when the sounds are blustering so loudly
that we can't ignore it,
what was once our best playlist life track now sounds
like noise.
our reality doesn't match the fantasy we lied to ourselves
about
and finally, we can behold truth
God flicks the switch back and wildly whips it forward
to the back of the head for a wakeup call

They come in all shapes and colors,
pain is always the base to the recipe,
the rest of the ingredients we added ourselves.
Now we have to demolish this meal
so the nutrients can thrive and morph us into our
newest character
All of sudden you realize nothing is the same
and it never will be again.
But is that a bad thing?!

2025. Fucked from the Start

I feel so heavy
Heavy in my thoughts
Heavy in my feelings
Heavy in my body
So consumed and filled with emptiness
I receive no nutrients from the food & drinks I eat
I receive no knowledge from what I choose to watch and
listen to
My mind races
and before I can decipher one thought
I'm on to the next
List of duties stacked
Resources lack
I'm in a position where I feel I'm in the middle of a scale
but not balanced
One move and everything collapses
Playing Jenga when I should be playing Tetris
But my life is not a game
I'm 32 and I need change
It's so scary because I've overcome so much

Little by little I've gained
what I once wanted and now that I have it
it's not enough
more maintaining

2020. Precarious

Quality time with self is a necessity
I am reminded of this, this very moment
To unwind, to balance, to access, to love, to value, to
remind me
I always feel as if it's this negative force over me,
One pulling me in and the other running away
So much responsibility is placed on my shoulders
Such high expectations set for myself
I'm not talking about bills, clothes, and hair
I'm talking about spiritual growth, mental expansion,
self-understanding, strategic planning and execution
Health and mental wellness.
No one else is to blame but me
I allow every interruption
and no one else understands or knows my journey but
me
I'm not regular
I'm not able to just live on a low frequency and never
look back
When I finally face my reflection

I'm quickly reminded of the being I set to the side
The one who yearns for me, whispers in my ear while
I'm sleeping,
Tugs at my heartstrings while I'm merely doing a
pointless activity
consumed in nothing

2020. Whispers in the Void

OUT
an escape from reality is what I yearn for
But there is no escape unless its death
I'm alive but damn sure not living
It's crazy because everytime I think of what defines
living
its surrounded by a world created by society
How can I focus on what makes me happy
if I have to mark off a list of to-do's
that are not in alignment with my purpose
Just to collect more materials to spend on "their" reality
Moving up a notch in status but many roles away from
true awareness
I seen a post the other day
in it was a lady standing in the middle of a moving
planet
and she was screaming
"pull over & let me out"
This shit is non stop
Before you can fix one issue, here come three more

You learn how to tackle & maintain
and then soon enough the dynamics shifts once again
I am gratefull
I was blessed with a new day to complete what I
couldn't yesterday
Still in my right mind & body that works perfectly fine
So cheers to tomorrow
May it be highlighted in change

2024. Status Quo Blues

How can I make this make sense?
Nothing truly does.
Everything I've ever known
seems to have a hint of a lie
or else, all it ever was
and will be
is just a façade.

What can I do
with these pieces
that never fit into the puzzle
to begin with?
Robbing Peter to pay Paul,
forever in debt over all.

How's money considered valuable
when the value of it ain't able?
How can we pick a president
for a government
that's supposed to provide stability

when the system it represents
ain't never been stable?

I'm just tired
of living in this fable.
Experiences and lessons—
same cycles,
different timetable.

I just want to breathe.
Find a space, and live.

I'm attached to so many things
that have no attachment to me.
I made no choice of my own to be.
There's no way to escape these thoughts.

I wish I was dumb and unaware
but that's not the case.
It's knowledge I have within,
that I have yet to tap into,
and don't even know how or if I want to.
Because what the fuck Ima do with it?

Everywhere I look is foul.
I know I was born for a reason,
but the purpose gets away from me

because I have to keep chasing
and maintaining
this false reality.

I'm tired.
I'm playing a game
I didn't sit down at the table for
on a board that was never meant for me to score.
The character I have to play with
ain't even relevant to my core.

The dice is in hand,
and I gotta shake
in hopes that the next move
gives me better bullshit to explore 🌚

2023. Pro-Black, Pro-What?

I feel confused
I want to be pro-black so bad
but what does that mean?
What does it represent —
and do I feel comfortable
with the representation representing me?
I want to be against police brutality
I want to be against violence in my neighborhood
I want to be kind
I want to love
I want to do what's right
But what is right anymore?
Will right protect me from wrong?
If I fight against the men in uniform
will I never call them for savior
from the very same people I wished to protect?
Everything I've ever known
is at odds with my current reality
If I think of other countries and how they live
I question if my whole life

has been a delusional dream
All the words that carry integrity, respect, community,
progression, evolution—
are built on the backs of deceit, manipulation, hatred,
and control
Even when I'm taking steps forward
it's in a backwards direction
And even if I'm in flow
I'm still within the same spin wheels of lies
I'm tired
but I can't give up
I want to fight
but I'm unsure of my opponent
What once represented strength
is buried beneath individual definitions
with empty purposes
I feel lost
and the scary part I'm accepting
is that this is an everlasting state of life
until my last breath
And if ever found—
under what pretenses?

2025. Stop Bleeding on Me

You're bleeding all over me,
N although I feel bad,
I no longer have the capacity to bandage you up.
I gave away my last band aid
And it's not in my budget to stock up.
No extra splints, syringes, IV's, or antibiotic creams,
All I have left is the bag on my back,
And everything in it is only for meeee.
Sorry I can't help you,
But please back up —
You're bleedinnggg all over me.
My wounds just began to mend,
My scars are starting to blend back into skin.
I'm showered, renewed, and smelling fresh.
My fit is nice and clean
And I don't want no leakage of yours coming from within.
It sounds harsh,
And I wish I could say I was sorry,
But when I was bruised and battered

All I had was my shadow
To pick me back up and guard me.
We got real close, no more divide.
Caught a good glimpse of myself from all sides.
My best friend became the image I used to flee,
She chased me down 'til I had no choice but to see.
When she caught me, the fog disappeared,
We opened my third eye,
Everything's crystal clear.
Now I can witness what you choose to ignore.
No worries, I get it, I been there before.
You got holes the size of trenches
They use in world wars.
You walk around cocky, head held high,
But if you were intentionally present for just a second
you would realize
That ya stride doesn't appear as strong as you believe.
That shit got a limp and its turning more into a lean
Thinking you dripping "that sauce", acting all pristine
But it's just bloody pus leaking from the wounds you
refuse to clean
Them bandages been warn out and you've lost all your
dressings
Even the best flex can't cover the pain you keep
suppressing
Your last martyr patched you up real well
You sucked them dry and watched them decay

Now you stand here exposed in the mess that you made
But facing yourself feels like too much to bear
So you run to me
Trying to talk that shit,
N show me your newest gear expecting for me to care
But I can't clap for confusion,
Can't toast with your narcissistic empty tears.
See, healing is not fashion
It doesn't come in new trends.
It's a war fought in silence,
Not staged for your friends.
You think I'm cold, detached, or acting brand new,
But I earned this peace, I bled for this view.
Had to crawl through my chaos,
Had to purge my own pain.
Now I guard my growth like crops after rain.
I ain't your savior
I'm not your nurse,
or your personal crutch,
My cup is finally full, can't keep pouring out too much.
So while you seek comfort, remember this plea:
You gotta stitch your own soul
Stop bleeding on me.

2023. Redemption for the Enemy within Me

I used to think of ways I could attempt to end my life
without pain

Staring into the well of darkness and imagining the
swiftest way to a quick efficient end
Tears rolling down my cheeks, landing on lips to afraid
and embarrassed to call a friend
No words to express, no energy to describe the feelings I
was so good with holding in.

I thought of using a razor to slice through my veins,
watching each red droplet fall until I could see no more
Or taking a bottle of pills and looking into the mirror
until I eventually dropped to the floor.
Maybe taking the train downtown and finding a tall
building to throw myself off of orrrr
Making a trip to homedepot for the strongest rope to tie
around my neck and jump from a high ceiling or even a
door

But as you can see I was unsuccessful with the actions
needed to follow through with my thoughts

At the time it was yet another reminder of the self-
disappointment and fears I was unconsciously taught
At age 35 I'm finally able to dissect each chapter of my
life
Page by page, word by word, letter by letter, trying to
find where I first encountered this strife
I go through many emotions, some sad, some happy,
some inbetween
But I see things different now, my survival, my struggles,
my experiences, all adding to this beautiful soul machine

However, I've realized suicide is still on the brain
I know, I know, give me a moment to explain

This time it's not physical, but more mental/spiritual to
say the least
This will take hard work, time, dedication, prayer
because baby I need the creator to help me kill this beast
Now the weapons are different no store to go to and buy
I hold them within but need some training and strength
which I know God will supply
This is years of abuse, neglect, and self-sabotage
It's not going to be easy this I know but this time
my revenge is brewing up the plan and it's my duty to

oblige

It's funny because Ive always felt I was in the gruesome
battle
Me vs me
And nothing had changed but this time I will have the
victory

So I was thinking of the first space I was in when I
picked up these self hatred manipulations
I realized that most insecurities developed through
unhealthy interactions
That plagued my spirit, and gave my internal gps
complications
Other peoples self projections they placed on my
shoulder and left me alone to mentally decipher and
digest the conversations
All these lyrical opinions from ppl that supposed to be
my family extensions play on my minds radio stations

But the voice echoing the lines in my head begins to
sound like mines
Before I knew it I allowed that shit to blur the lines

Daddy's liquor bought out a sermon, wrapped in gospels
of my pain,
he preached with slurred scriptures, that tore me down

time and time again
The first man I ever loved taught me why its not a safe
place
Because love hurts and can keep you tangled in a very
low state

Mama pressed me about perfection, and I never fit that
mold
Cuz perfection is a just a prison with bars dripped in
gold
She meant to shield me from the world but locked me in
my head
So I processed my emotions in silence more than
speaking what my mind said

I used to believe in deep sisterhood, finding and keeping
every connection I could
I told secrets believing they would keep them just to be
disappointed and bruised.
Fake friends wore smiles but sharpened their blades,
fed off my doubt while my confidence in the definition
slowly decayed.

I laid down like a sacrifice for men who only took,
gave them chapters of my body when they never read
the book.
I called it loyalty, devotion, even love in disguise—

but it was hunger in their hands, and starvation in my
eyes

See, I was raised in a bubble where the air was too clean,
no street fight lessons, no sharpened teeth, just a
sheltered dream.
So when life cut me open, I bled innocence and trust,
had to stitch my wounds with affirmations scribbled on
dust.

Now I'm breaking radios that replay their lies,
I'm muting every voice that taught me compromise.
I dig graves for projections, bury shame in the ground,
resurrecting only truth and I love how it sound.

Now hear me: I don't answer anger with the same old
pain,
I don't become their echo or rehearse their cruel refrain.
I find the source, unpick the seam, expose the how and
why,
I take their sentences apart and watch their meanings
die.

I strip the labels off my skin — "not enough," "too wide,"
"too small,"
I fold them up and feed them to the flame until their
voices fall.

I pull the cords that tuned my ear to radios that looped
their lies,
I change the channel to my voice and teach my mouth to
rise.

I am my muse and Messiah, I'm the weapon and womb,
a crown made of fire, commanding the room.
And the ones who once fed on my sorrow and cries—
are left choking on silence while I prophesy.

This is confidence roaring, this is purpose reborn,
this is venom and honey, the rose and the thorn.
And if you doubt me, step close and you'll see,
I was birthed for this throne — and the throne births me.